Peculiar Rhymes and Lunatic Lines

BY MAX FATCHEN

with illustrations by Lesley Bisseker.

ORCHARD BOOKS

For Rosie and Rebecca
M.F.

ORCHARD BOOKS
96 Leonard Street, London EC2A 4RH
Orchard Books, Australia
14 Mars Road, Lane Cove, NSW 2066
1 85213 885 8
First published in Great Britain in 1995
The right of Max Fatchen to be identified as the author and Lesley Bisseker as the illustrator of this work has been asserted by them in accordance with the Copyright, Designs and Patents Act, 1988.
A CIP catalogue record for this book is available from the British Library.
Printed and bound in Great Britain by
Bookcraft (Bath) Ltd.

Inside this book you will find extremely lunatic lines on everything and anything including:

All About ME (on page 6)

All about my family (try page 21)

School Scribbles (refer to page 31)

Notes on Nibbling (dig into page 45)

Some curious Creatures, (crawling around page 53)

Spotted at sports (on, under and over page 62)

Thoughts on friends and Things (from page 71 till the END.)

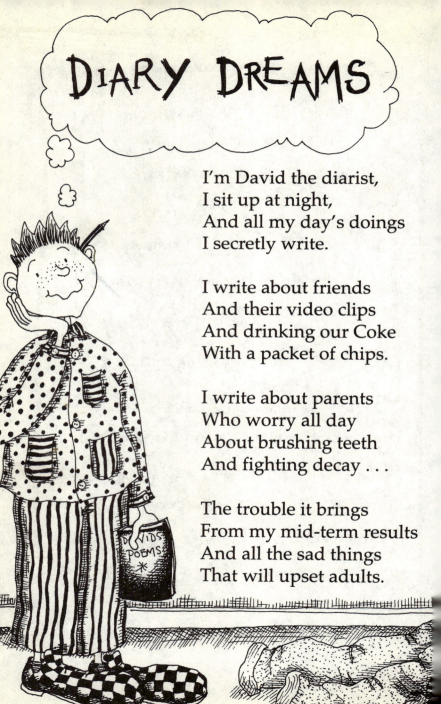

DIARY DREAMS

I'm David the diarist,
I sit up at night,
And all my day's doings
I secretly write.

I write about friends
And their video clips
And drinking our Coke
With a packet of chips.

I write about parents
Who worry all day
About brushing teeth
And fighting decay . . .

The trouble it brings
From my mid-term results
And all the sad things
That will upset adults.

So all my adventures
I've carefully stored,
Of when I felt happy
And how I felt bored.

So when the cats creep
And the telly's turned low
And the street seems asleep,
Then I let the words flow . . .

On to the paper
And out of my head,
Writing my thoughts
As I sit up in bed . . .

Writing and writing,
Line after line,
A diary's exciting,
Especially mine.

I like small kittens, budgerigars and pups,
But I'm not so keen on grown-ups.

ALL ABOUT ME

Why is it when I'm sitting still,
My parents ask me if I'm ill?

I know that face

Where's your pride?
Have you none?
Shoes untied,
Coat undone.
Grubby cheeks
For all to see . . .
Mirror, mirror . . .
HEY . . . that's me!

ER, HELLO

It's manners to rise
When visitors come
But hard when I've sat
On chewing gum

LOSING LOOKS

Making ugly faces
Is better left alone.
It's such disgrace
To pull a face
That's better than your own!

WELL, YOU SEE . . .

My lumps
And bumps
Are caused by thumps
But also
By mumps.

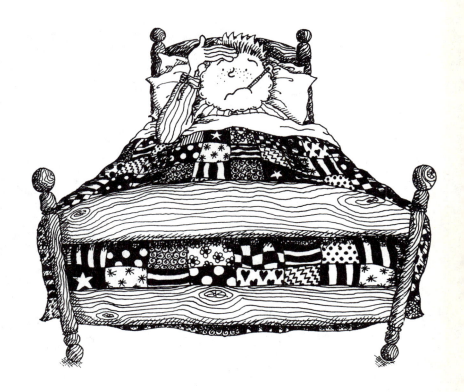

BODY BITS

If recycling makes things useful again,
Why not recycle my sister's brain?

Your eyes are blue
And mine are not.
With soap in them
They go bloodshot.

When you grow older
Chins grow bolder,
And cause trouble
By turning double.

Mouths are for opening wide
So dentists can peer inside.

Hands can be slender,
Charming or chubby,
Shapely or tender,
But mostly they're grubby.

Some stomachs are flat,
and some are round,
While empty ones
Make a rumbling sound.

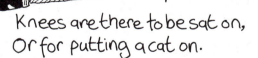

Knees are there to be sat on,
Or for putting a cat on.

Don't you think it's nice and neat
How toes and legs are joined to feet.
And rather clever, as you'll see,
The way they join the rest of me?

GROWING

The people whom I always dread
Are those who pat me on the head
And use a condescending tone,
"My goodness, child, and how you've
    g r o w n."
They tell my mother, "Dear, it's true,
He's growing more and more like you."
That's odd. As far as I can see,
I'm only growing more like me.

EMPTY POCKET POEM

If I get your slippers
And make tea,
Could you possibly . . .
Would I dare risk it . . .
That's if I add your favourite biscuit
And pour you a second cup
To follow up
After asking how was your day,
Could you possibly see your way . . .
I mean, is there any chance . . .
Of a small advance?

FOR INSTANCE

I can't stand people who won't share
But when I'm spending MY money
They are ALWAYS there.
I dislike people who borrow skateboards
   and scooters
Or MY video games for their computers.
Or people who say I'm too thin,
Who never knock but walk straight in,
Who won't go on hikes because it's too far
Or say they'll be here at a certain time
   but never are.
They're people I just can't stand.
On the other hand —
And I'm sure you'll agree —
There are some people
Who are really nice

For instance, there's me!

BE REASONABLE

Untidiness
Can make a mess
But neatness
Brings sweetness.
Then why make a scene
If I'm halfway between?

IT JUST HAPPENS

When I've packed my case
And used every space,
Then fastened the straps,
I always have this doubt:
I've left something out.
Has it happened to you?

When my teacher says,
"Don't forget your homework book,"
And I get home and look,
I go out of my mind.
Guess what I've left behind?

When I pin notes on my shelf
To remind myself,
Or tie my wrists with strings
To remember things,
It's quite a surprise
And my head starts to whizz
When somebody cries,
"Do you know what day this is?"
But I never do.
Has it happened to you?

KITE DREAMS

If I were a kite
I'd swoop down the sky,
In airy delight
I'd flutter and fly.
Lifting and shifting,
I'd swing and I'd sail,
Flagging and wagging
My colourful tail.
I'd dart and I'd dive,
I'd fly and I'd fling.
Instead I'm just holding
This silly old
string.

AHOY

If I were a sailor
I'd climb a high mast,
While swaying and watching
The ships going past . . .
I'd wave to the seagulls
Then pause with a frown.
When you climb a high mast
You have to climb down.

I'm David, nine and nearly ten.
I know that boys grow into men.
But if I reach a hundred and twenty,
Then I'll consider that is plenty.

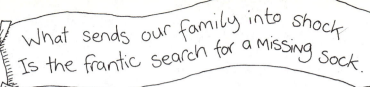

What sends our family into shock
Is the frantic search for a missing sock.

ALL ABOUT MY FAMILY

What makes our family fly into rages
Is people who stay in the bathroom for ages.

SISTER SOUNDS

I can't understand it,
Can you?
But it's true
That whales are enormous.
Yet they speak
With a tiny squeal
And a gentle squeak.
But my sister,
Who's only two,
Makes the most awful
Hullaballoo.

I can't understand it,
Can you?

(big mouth).

BROTHER BOTHER

My brother doesn't wash his face,
His hair is never trim.
My brother's not afraid of germs
But they're afraid of him.

I showed my brother the shining stars.
I thought it was a favour.
I pointed out the Milky Way,
He stared and said: "What flavour?"

WATCH IT

A mother is wise,
So people have said,
And seems to have eyes in the back
of her head.
But I'll be honest,
And I'll be blunt,
My mother sees plenty
From hers in front.

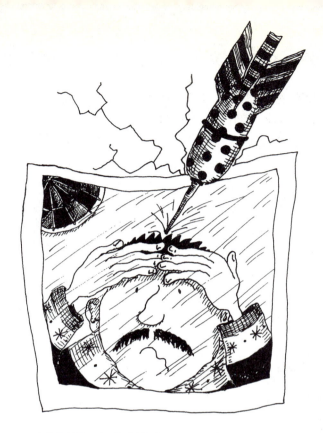

MISSED AGAIN

My father's not terribly smart
At hitting a board with a dart.
It's rather a shame
That, when he takes aim,
People lie on the floor or depart.

HOTROD DOG

Now when we drive the family car
We rattle and roar and chug,
But our dog wants a window seat
And our dog wants the rug.

Our dog barks impatiently,
That's if we drive too slow.
Our dog whines at the traffic lights
Until the green says go.

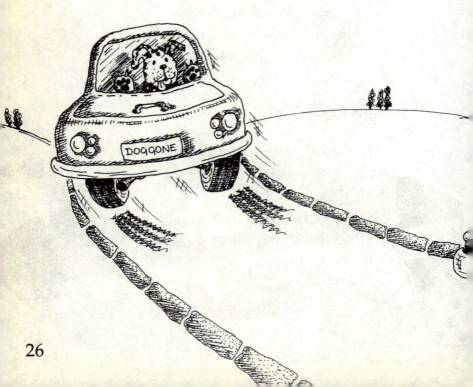

Our dog watches the lorries pass
While vans are his delight.
He barks when we are veering left,
He yaps when we turn right.

His whining and his yelping make
My father lose his head.
No wonder that he didn't see
The traffic light turn red.

The cruising police patrol will glare.
My father's no road hog.
He simply says he cannot bear
Our back-seat driving dog.

BE CAREFUL OF COUSINS

When cousin Jeremy was one
He crawled into a drain for fun.

 When cousin Jeremy was two
He did the things you shouldn't do.

When cousin Jeremy was three
He poured the cat's milk in the tea.

 When Jeremy was barely four
I didn't like him any more.

At five he played such awful tricks
Which lasted till the age of six.

 From seven, until nearly eight,
Our mother said he tempted fate
Especially when at naughty nine
He pegged my sister on the line.

This ghastly news I now must pen,
Tomorrow JEREMY IS TEN!

It isn't any wonder that
My cousin Clive is feeling flat.
The trouble with this careless stroller,
He never saw the council roller.

AS LONG AS THEY DO

I get so exasperated
With people to whom I'm related,
But I'm ready to praise
If they remember birthdays.

COOL CAT

Our cat sleeps all day
Which is cool.
But my teachers say
That's what I do
At school.

RUSHING

Rush, rush,
Race, race.
Teeth to brush,
Wash your face.

Eat your toast,
Drink your cup.
For goodness' sake,
Hurry up.

Where's my bag?
On the chair.
Quick, quick,
Comb your hair.

Shoes done,
Fuss, fuss.
Run, run,
School bus.

Books turn.
Weary brain,
Learn, learn.
Home again.

It's wonderful
To laze away,
Sleeping in
On Saturday.

z z z z

SO THIN

This
is
a
verse
that's
very
thin.
I
hope
that
I
can
get
it
in.
I
wish
that
I
could

it.
Instead
I think I'll **Flatten** it.

WELL, ISN'T IT?

Homework
Is given to children
Who would like to shun it.

Homework
Is given to children
So parents can say,
"Have you done it?"

IT FIGURES

My calculator is my friend,
The very best of chums.
It likes to please,
I press its keys
And watch it do my sums.

WHERE'S THAT?

Geography is never for me
And causes my teachers to sigh.
I certainly know
That Holland's quite low,
Mount Everest is terribly high.

The rivers that wind
I never can find
Whenever I'm put to the test.
Now Scotland's up north
With the Firth of the Forth,
America's somewhere out west.

I'm puzzled and dull
When searching for Hull
And cities like Rio and Rome.
My teacher will fret
That I can't find Tibet
But at least I can find my way home.

TEACHER TORMENT

Pay attention, David.
Pay attention, Sue.
Albert, stop that talking!
We have things to do.

I can hear a murmur.
PLEASE, all concentrate.
Would you stop, Vanessa,
Whispering to Kate?

George, would you mind reading
And leave the girls alone?
Pay attention, David,
Stop distracting Joan.

Jeremy, I'm worried
Your vocal cords will strain.
Could you spare a moment
From gossiping with Jane?

Natter . . . natter . . . natter,
No wonder teachers scold.
As champions of chatter
You'd win Olympic gold!

Did you know that the high-hovering hawk
Can spy tiny creatures in the grass
Nearly as quickly as my teacher can spot
People eating potato crisps in class.

SCRAPS

Yum Yum!

What, no cream buns in the school canteen?
No wonder I feel frustrated and mean.

There's too much bossing
At our school crossing.

Paper and trees, Don't waste them please.

Q – What's worse than tigers and lions that growl?

A – It's our teacher on the prowl.

EXCURSIONS

Going on excursions,
Riding in a bus,
Teacher busy counting
Every one of us.

Pointing at the landscape
As we go along,
Shouting at each other,
Breaking into song.

Unloading at the seaside,
Teacher gives advice.
Someone's pulling faces
Which isn't very nice.

Eating at the kiosk,
Listening to the band,
Leaping over puddles,
Somersaults on sand.

Someone has a nosebleed.
Someone stubs a toe.
Teacher giving first aid,
Rushing to and fro.

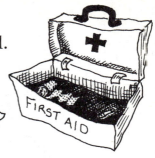

Day's excursion over.
Good things always end.
Fighting for the window,
Sitting with a friend.

Teacher tired and grumpy.
Such a day of fun.
Any missing children?
What a shame — not one!

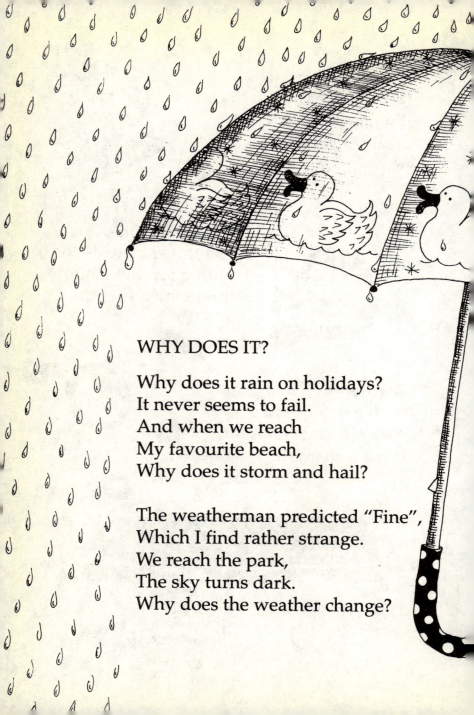

WHY DOES IT?

Why does it rain on holidays?
It never seems to fail.
And when we reach
My favourite beach,
Why does it storm and hail?

The weatherman predicted "Fine",
Which I find rather strange.
We reach the park,
The sky turns dark.
Why does the weather change?

What's happened to a pleasant day?
The clouds will leak and drip.
The blizzards blow
With sleet and snow,
When teachers plan our trip.

But when I'm hard at work in school,
I want to scream and shout,
It's as I feared,
The sky has cleared,
And look ... the sun is out!

Brain diminished,
Exam finished.

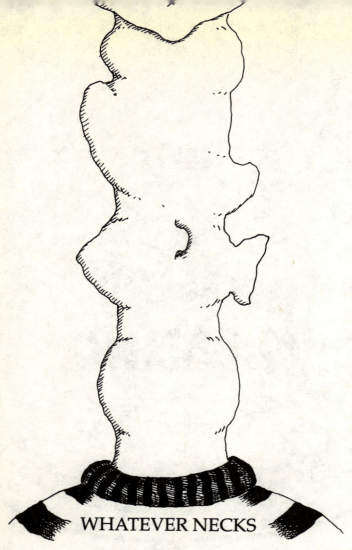

WHATEVER NECKS

It's just as well
That necks are hollow,
For otherwise
How would we swallow?

YES P-L-E-A-S-E

Would you like
an all-colours-of-the-rainbow
ice-cream
with specks
of peppermint
chocolate
dotted with raisins
resting
in a great blob
of cream
on top
of a crusty,
crunchy,
munchy,
melt-in-the-mouth
apple pie,
this high?

So nobody will hear,
I'll whisper in your ear.

So would I.

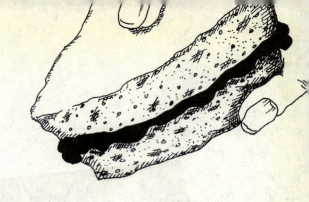

WHAT, NOT EVEN A CRUMB?

Isn't it sickly
That people eat so quickly
When they dine.
Because, make no mistake,
That last piece of cake
Was really mine.

MILKSHAKE

Whizz,
spin,
milky
din.
Twirl,
whirl,
gurgling
sound.
Mixer
spinning
round
and
round.
Strawberry
broth
foaming
froth.
Scarlet
drips.
Licking
lips.
Whizz,
spin,
end
of din.
Pass
glass.

Straw in.

A meal cooked by boys?
With praise we should greet it.
It's finding someone
Who's willing to eat it.

What interferes with pleasure and play?
Why, wiping dishes and putting them away.

AND NOT BEFORE TIME

Takeaway food
Brings takeaway glee,
But when I want more
They take away me.

SO SIMPLE

Here's a riddle fresh from space,
It came with bleeps and blips.
What does a Martian have for lunch?
Why, fish and micro-chips.

ALWAYS BUSY

Busy tastebuds never shirk
And mine are pleased at so much work.
They never pause to take a stroll.
So here's another sausage roll.

SPLOSH!

Spaghetti's clinging to my fork,
A squirming mass it makes.
With aching wrist,
I turn and twist,
It writhes like little snakes.
Spaghetti's difficult to eat,
I twirl it round and round.
A splash! Oh dear!
Please all stand clear
For now it's come unwound!

Roosters crow when day is dawning.
The rest of us just lie there yawning.

Some Curious Creatures

Bubbles in Streams

Could be frogs having dreams.

A turtle doesn't hurtle,
And why worry
When there's no hurry.

READ ALL ABOUT IT

The newt
Can scoot,
I understand,
Under water
Or on land.
I know about
this clever caper,
I read it in
Today's newts' paper.

SPOTS

Leopards have them,
Clouds can shake them.
Measles bring them,
Ink can make them.
You twitch
As they itch
With irritation.
But they don't seem to worry
Our Dalmatian.

DINOSORE

The dinosaur, a creature strong,
Was far too big and far too long.

No wonder it could never smile,

With backache stretching half a mile.

DO BE CAREFUL

A charmer of snakes it must irk
When his python goes really berserk.
It crushes him tightly
But, though it's unsightly,
At least he's wrapped up
    in his work.

A saucy young mermaid, Miranda,
Was flattered by efforts to land her.
She was lured to a net
Which she lived to regret
For they took her ashore and then cannned her.

Hibernation in winter's the thing
And a habit to which bears will cling.
Say the bears with a shrug,
"If you're wanting a hug
You'd better come back in the spring."

AND BEHIND YOUR EARS, TOO

A mother hippopotamus,
Her voice both calm
    and steady,
Said: "Do come here,
It's bathtime, dear.
I've got your river ready."

FOOTSORE

The centipede will always choose
To run around without its shoes,
But does it, when the day's expired,
Put all its feet up when it's tired?

ODD ANTICS

A garden ant I've come to know
Has gone to book with P & O.
It wants to sail the seven seas
And visit the ANTipodes.

WHAT A BLOW!

An elephant's gigantic sneeze,
A monstrous A-A-A-R-R-T-I-S-H-O-O-O-O-O !
Has all the keepers, so I'm told,
Now searching for the zoo.

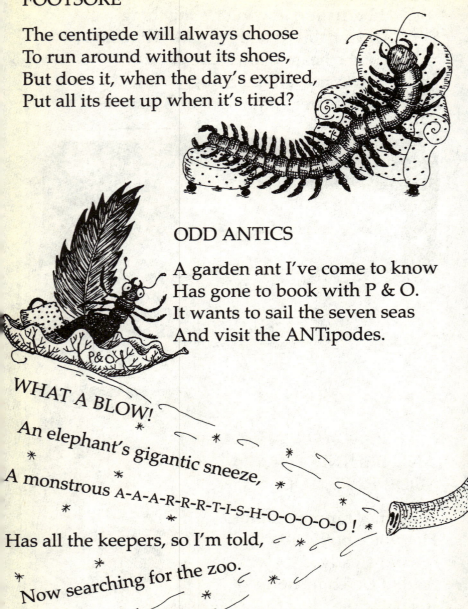

THE PRISONER

Little crab that I've caught
On the rim of the tide,
You nip and you drip,
You struggle and slide.
Although you look fierce,
I think I can tell,
Your small brain is timid
Beneath your hard shell.
You struggle and crawl,
Now you're safe on the sands,
And back to the sea
From my prison of hands.

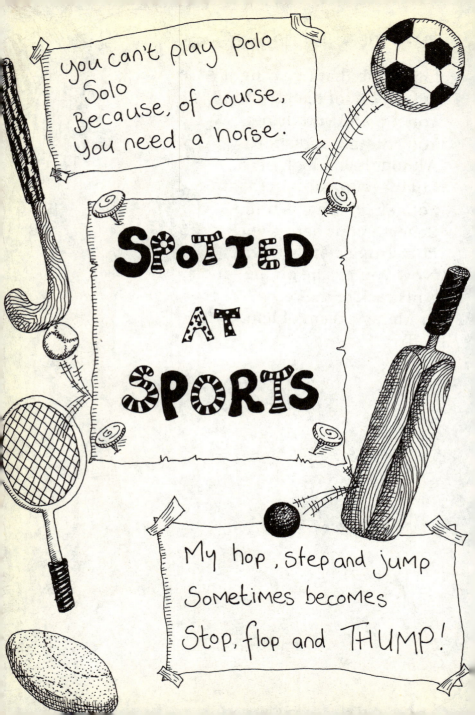

Gerald did a high jump,
A boastful boy is he.
He went too high
And that is why
He's caught up in that tree.

Three-legged races
Make you stumble,
Trip and fall,
S p r a w l
And tumble
With pains from sprains.
Unless you're tough
I think two legs
Are quite enough.

CRICKET CALAMITY

Some cricketers
Are at a loss
With a full toss
As it's soaring
For scoring
And bending
And descending.
They try
To give it thumps
With their bat
But it hits the stumps

OWZAT!

SOMERSAULTS

Turning a somersault's
Nimble and neat.
You curve through the air
And you land on your feet.

Is it a rocket Saturn-bound,
A plane that's reached the speed of sound,
This flying object that we've seen?
It's Tessa . . . on the trampoline.

CATASTROPHE

Roller-skate
Fast rate
TOO LATE
No gate!

GOAL GLORY

I kicked a goal! I kicked a goal!
I struck it fair and square.
And like a hurtling meteorite,
The ball whizzed through the air.

The goalie leapt, but all in vain,
And fell upon his face.
And joy went throbbing through my brain,
My pulse began to race.

I kicked a goal! I kicked a goal!
With others shouting, "Shoot!"
And faster than a rocket ship,
The ball went from my boot.

My team-mates hugged me with delight,
I wished we'd been on telly.
My heart was beating like a drum,
My kneecaps turned to jelly.

"He kicked a goal," the gruff coach said.
"We're on a winning streak.
He's got some sense in that young head,
Select him for next week."

SUCH A RACQUET

Whack· · · · · · ·crack,
There · · · and · · · back,
Whizzing · · · to and fro.
Swinging · · · swerving,
Sizzling · · · · serving,
Hitting *high* · and low.
Lashing · · · · crashing,
Dashing · · · smashing,
Hear the linesman's call.
Belted · · · · · · · spun,
There's not much fun,
When you're a tennis ball.

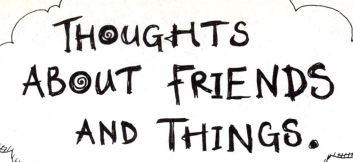

IF ONLY...

If I could work magic
I'd take you away
To a land where there wasn't
A single dull day.

No viewers who switched
To their programmes instead.
No people who scolded
At clothes on your bed...

Who twisted their faces
A terrible shape
Because you kept playing
Your top ten on tape.

There'd not be a racket
Or making those scenes
At spots on your jacket
Or holes in your jeans.

We'd go to the fairgrounds
Or walk on the piers.
We'd eat our fast foods
And sip ginger beers.

With chocolates for breakfast
And visits to zoos,
With no one who wanted
The BBC news.

If I could work magic
I certainly would,
And you'd be invited
If ONLY I could.

DIVE AND DIP

Rise and rip, dive and dip, leaning backwards with the strain.
Rattling, roaring, upward soaring, swirling, whirling in your brain.
Looping, lunging, downward plunging, going round a dizzy bend.

Swinging, clinging, heads are ringing, holding tightly to a friend.
Hands that clasp, scream and gasp, funny feelings here inside.
Ears are popping now we're stopping.
That's a roller coaster ride.

WAVING

You passed in a car
As onward it sped.
I saw your quick smile,
The turn of your head.

I knew that you cared . . .
That smile you had saved
For the moment you spared
When you saw me and waved.

ISN'T IT AMAZING?

Now isn't it amazing
That seeds grow into flowers,
That grubs become bright butterflies
And rainbows come from showers,
That busy bees make honey gold
And never spend time lazing,
That eggs turn into singing birds,
Now isn't that amazing?

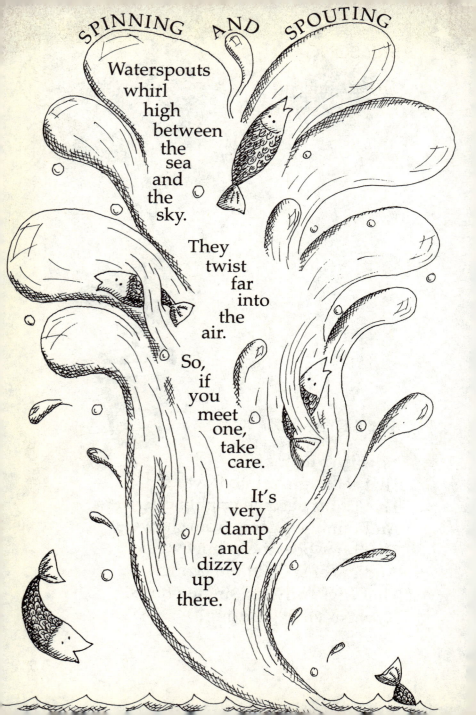

SKY SONG

The setting sun
Has such surprises,
For when it sets
Somewhere it rises.

ADVICE TO A SPACE SHUTTLE

Don't hijack the moon
Wherever you steer,
For people like me
Need moonbeams down here.

AND THAT'S ALL

A happy day
Is precious to keep
So take it to bed
And wrap it in sleep.